Indian Nations

THE CHEROKEE

by
Herb McAmis

General Editors
Herman J. Viola and Felix C. Lowe

A Rivilo Book

RSVP
RAINTREE STECK-VAUGHN
PUBLISHERS
A Steck-Vaughn Company

Austin, Texas
www.steck-vaughn.com

Published by Raintree Steck-Vaughn Publishers, an imprint of the Steck-Vaughn Company

Developed for Steck-Vaughn Company by Rivilo Books, Bluffton, SC

Editor: Jan Danis

Photo Research: William A. Eames and Paula Dailey

Design: Barbara Lisenby and Todd Hirshman

Electronic Preparation: Curry Printing

Raintree Steck-Vaughn Publishers Staff

Publishing Director: Walter Kossmann

Editor: Kathy DeVico

Design Project Manager: Lyda Guz

Photo Credits: Franklin Shipe: cover, pp. 18, 23, 25 bottom, 26, 35; Lisa Ranallo Horse Capture: illustration, pp. 4, 6; Michael Kesselring: 7, 24 top, 36, 43; Herb McAmis: pp. 9 top, 20, 24 bottom, 33; Richard Alexander Cooke III/NGS Image Collection: pp. 9 bottom, 41 bottom; Smithsonian Archives : p. 13 (from a painting by Charles B. King), 21; Woolaroc Museum, Bartlesville, Oklahoma: p. 15 ("The Trail of Tears" by Robert Lindneux, 1942); Courtesy of Cherokee Tribal Travel and Promotion Office, David Redman: pp. 16, 22, 38; Courtesy of Doug Conner: p. 19; George F. Mobley/NGS Image Sales: p. 25 right; Jim Blair/NGS Image Sales: p. 27; Randy Olson/NGS Image Sales: p. 29; Maggie Steber: pp. 28, 30, 31, 34, 41 top; Library of Congress: p. 40; Mark Finchum, Jefferson City, Tenn.: p. 42. The following images were photographed courtesy of the Cherokee Heritage Museum and Gallery in Cherokee, North Carolina (CHMG), Dr. Michael and Susan Abram, Directors, and the Cherokee Heritage Center in Tahlequah, Oklahoma: cover (coat by William Loffiah), pp. 7 (figures by Charlie Reed and wolf and basket by Virgile Crowe), 20, 23, 24 top (doll by Betty Lossiah), 25 left, 26, 35, 36 (mask by Larry Armachain), 43 (made by John Wilnoty, Jr.)

Library of Congress Cataloging-in-Publication Data

McAmis, Herb.

    The Cherokee / by Herb McAmis.

      p.   cm. — (Indian nations)

    "A Rivilo book."

    Includes bibliographical references.

    Summary: Tells about the history and culture of the Cherokee, explains how European explorers affected the society of this Indian people, and looks into their future.

    ISBN 0-8172-5456-0

    1. Cherokee Indians — History Juvenile literature.   2. Cherokee Indians — Government relations Juvenile literature.   3. Cherokee Indians — Social life and customs Juvenile literature.   [1. Cherokee Indians.   2. Indians of North America — Southern States.]   I. Title. II. Series: Indian nations (Austin, Tex.)

E99.C5M37   2000   99-23093

975'.0049755 — dc21   CIP

Printed and bound in the United States of America

1 2 3 4 5 6 7 8 9 0 LB 03 02 01 00 99

Contents

Cherokee Legends and Folktales

How the Earth Was Made

"This is what the old men told me when I was a boy." (This is the way all Cherokee stories begin.) Once there was nothing but water all over the world. All the animals were living above the blue sky dome, or "Sky Rock," which the Cherokee call Galun'lati, meaning "above on high." It was getting very crowded there. So the animals decided to send one of their number down to see what was under the water.

At last Dayunisi, the little water beetle, offered to go and see. It darted about over the surface of the water but could find no dry land. Then it dived to the bottom and came up with a little bit of soft mud. The mud began to grow and spread until it became the island we call Earth. It was floating on the water, held up by four cords. There was a cord at each direction—north, south, east, and west—attached to the great, blue Sky Rock.

At first the earth was all flat and very soft and wet. The animals sent different birds down to see if it was dry yet. None of them could find a dry place to alight, so they returned to Galun'lati. At last they sent the great buzzard, the father of all buzzards living today. He flew down to find a place for the animals to live. He flew all over the earth, very low, down near the ground. When he reached what became Cherokee country, he

◄ When water covered the world, Dayunisi, the water beetle, brought a speck of soft mud from the bottom. The mud grew and grew until it formed the Earth.

5

was very tired. His wings began to strike the soft ground. Wherever his wings hit the earth, there was a valley. Where his wings turned up again there was a mountain. The animals were afraid the whole world would become mountains, so they called the buzzard back. That is why the Cherokee country is full of mountains to this day.

Animals and Plants

This is what the old men told me when I was a boy: All the animals and plants were told to watch and to stay awake for seven days and nights. They all tried very hard. After the first night, most of them were still awake. The next night, several dropped off to sleep. On the third night still others slept, and each night several more. On the seventh night, only the owl, the panther, and one or two others were still awake. These animals were given the power to see and to go about in the dark. They were also allowed to feed upon birds and animals who must sleep at night. Of all the trees, only the cedar, the pine, the spruce, the holly, and the laurel were awake on the seventh night. To them was given the power always to stay green and to be used for medicine. All the others must lose all their hair (leaves) every winter.

People Are Made

This is what the old men told me when I was a boy: After the animals and plants were on the Earth, people were made. At first there were only two. Their names were Kanati and Selu. Then Kanati struck Selu with a fish and told her to multiply, and so it was. In seven days a child was born to her. Every seven days after that, another child was born. The children increased so fast there was danger that the world could not hold them. Ever since then, a woman can have only one child a year. Kanati became the father of successful hunters, and Selu is known as "the mother of corn."

Kanati (right) is the father of hunting, and Selu (left) is the mother of corn.

Prehistory

Origin of the Cherokees

The area where the Cherokee Tribe began was on a tributary of the Ohio River near what is now Pittsburgh, Pennsylvania. In this part of the country, there are many caves. Other tribes who lived nearby often called the ancestors of the Cherokee people "cave people" and said they had come up out of the ground.

The name by which the Cherokee first called themselves was Ani Yunwiya, meaning "the principal people." The word "Cherokee" has no meaning in their own language, so it must be a **foreign** word.

If you ask a Cherokee today, "What is your tribe?" he or she will probably answer, "I am **Tsalagi**" (sa la gee'). Sometimes they call themselves Ani Kituwah, (Ah nee - Gi doo' wa), meaning "people of Kituwah." This was the name of one of their first large settlements in the area we know today as Cherokee country.

Migration Story

After some battles with other tribes, the Cherokees began to move south. Legends say they lived for "a long time" around the Peaks of Otter, near what is now Charlottesville, Virginia. Still their old enemies sent war parties to fight them. The Cherokees moved farther south to escape these constant conflicts. Their first settlement in what came to be known as "Cherokee country" was on the Nolichucky River in what became eastern Tennessee. The Cherokees called this river, *Nana tlu gunyi*, which means "spruce tree place." John Haywood wrote that a

Banks of the Nolichucky River in eastern Tennessee held the first settlement in what is now called "Cherokee Country."

tribal elder once told him that "...they had lived there so long that no one then alive could remember living anywhere else."

Finally, the Cherokees moved still farther south and built their first southern capital town of Tanasi. The very name of the state of Tennessee comes from the Cherokee town Tanasi. Later, during colonial times, the Cherokee capital town was Chota. It was on the Little Tennessee River near the present city of Loudon, Tennessee.

In the 1700s the Cherokee capital, Chota, was on the Little Tennessee River before it was flooded by a dam.

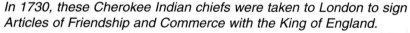

Key Historical Events

First European Contacts

The first known contact between the Cherokees and whites was in 1540, when Spanish explorer Hernando de Soto marched his army into Cherokee territory searching for gold. We know there was gold in the Cherokee territory. Fortunately, de Soto did not find it. Instead, he hurried on south and west into Creek Indian territory. In 1629 Cornelius Dougherty, an Irishman from Virginia, became the first white trader to live among the Cherokees. Not long after Charleston, South Carolina, was settled in 1670, English traders became a fairly common sight among the Cherokees.

In 1730 Sir Alexander Cuming took seven Cherokee chiefs and subchiefs with him to England to meet the king. The English nicknamed one of these chiefs Attakullakulla, which means "little carpenter." They said he could make the two sides of a dispute fit together like a fine carpenter's joint. He became the most famous Cherokee peace chief. While in England, these

In 1730, these Cherokee Indian chiefs were taken to London to sign Articles of Friendship and Commerce with the King of England.

chiefs signed a "treaty of friendship" with the British, which the tribe never broke. The Cherokees kept their word and supported the English, even fighting against the colonists who were striving for freedom during the American Revolution.

Trade with Europeans brought many changes to the Cherokees. The best new items that they acquired were iron tools and cooking vessels, which worked much better than stone tools and clay pots. To get these new items, the Cherokees had to trade deer and other animal skins to the whites for the desired European goods. This caused the Cherokees to do something they had never done before, something that was forbidden by their religion. They killed more deer than they needed to feed and clothe themselves.

White traders also brought guns and ammunition, so the Cherokees could kill still more deer. Soon the deer and bear near their towns became scarce. The Cherokees had to roam farther and farther from home to find game. This often left their wives, children, and elders unprotected from their enemies, both white and Indian.

The whites also brought European diseases. The Indians had no **immunity** to these. A smallpox **epidemic** killed almost half the Cherokees in one year. Other diseases such as measles, chicken pox, and whooping cough often killed Indian people, but nothing was as deadly as smallpox. Some who survived committed suicide when they saw the scars this disease left on their bodies.

The Europeans also introduced rum and other alcoholic drinks, which the Cherokees had never tasted before. Many chiefs begged the whites not to trade rum to their people, but the whites did not stop. They could take more advantage of a drunken Indian when trading.

White Men's Wars

Throughout the colonial period, Britain, France, and Spain tried to gain control of North America. They used every possible method to get the Indian tribes to help one of them against the other two. During the French and Indian War, the Creeks, the Cherokees' neighbors and bitter enemies to the south, were loyal to the French. When the British finally defeated the French and won control of all of eastern North America in 1763, the Cherokees thought that their troubles were over. The British passed a law that no white settler could move west of the crest of the Allegheny Mountains. In spite of this law, however, American colonists continued to pour across the mountains into what are now Tennessee and Kentucky. The British did not try to stop them.

The American Revolution

After the Americans defeated the British in 1783, they demanded even more Cherokee land than had the British. The Cherokees decided that if they adopted the white man's way of life, they could become a part of the new nation. Along with the Chickasaws, Choctaws, Creeks, and Seminoles, they adapted so well that together they became known as "the five civilized tribes." This made no difference. The whites still wanted all of their lands.

The War of 1812

The War of 1812 was fought between Britain and America. In 1813 the British helped a **radical** group of Creeks, known as the "Red Sticks," to take the warpath against the United States. The Red Sticks attacked Fort Mims in southern Alabama, killing more than 350 Americans.

In 1814 General Andrew Jackson led a large force against the Red Stick Creeks. His army included many Cherokee warriors. Finally, they surrounded most of the Creeks at Horseshoe Bend on the Tallapoosa River. A bloody battle raged for hours. First one side and then the other seemed to be winning. In the end, a furious Cherokee charge gave Jackson the victory.

Cherokees Develop a Written Language

In 1809 Sequoyah, a Cherokee whose English name was George Gist (or Guess), realized that the Cherokees needed to be able to read and write. This would help them in dealing with the whites. Sequoyah developed a system of writing the Cherokee language. It was a **syllabary** made up of 85 characters. The Cherokee National Council officially adopted it in 1821. It was the first written Indian language in North America.

Sequoyah's syllabary worked like an alphabet, except that each symbol stood for a sound in the Cherokee language. Cherokees didn't have to learn to spell because the symbols stood for sounds, not letters. Within three years, about three-fourths of their people could read and write Cherokee. Soon there was a Cherokee newspaper.

Sequoyah (left) whose mother was Cherokee and whose father was English, developed a syllabary or alphabet (above) so that his people might learn to read.

Conflict with Georgia

In 1829 gold was discovered on Cherokee lands in what is now northeast Georgia. Whites poured into this forbidden area looking for gold. The state of Georgia illegally claimed this land. Its legislature passed laws that made it a crime for Cherokees to mine gold on their own land. Neither could they **testify** in court against a white man nor hold political assemblies. The Cherokee government could no longer function in Georgia.

John Ross (or Gu'wisguwi') was the principal chief of the Cherokees at that time. He went with a group of Cherokee leaders to Washington, D.C., to protest the Georgia laws as a violation of many treaties with the United States. Both Congress and President Andrew Jackson ignored them. At last, the Cherokees took their case against Georgia to the Supreme Court of the United States. Chief Justice John Marshall and the Supreme Court ruled for the Cherokees. When he heard this, President Jackson is said to have remarked, "John Marshall has made his ruling. Now let him enforce it!" Of course, since he had no troops under his command, Justice Marshall could not enforce the court's decision. So the state of Georgia sent the **militia** to drive the Cherokees out of their homes. They took the Cherokees' houses, furniture, farms, animals, crops, and tools. Some Cherokees were able to keep only the clothes they were wearing. The U.S. government did nothing to stop this violence.

The Trail of Tears

Andrew Jackson owed a huge debt to the Cherokees, even his life. Still, after he was elected president in 1828, he pushed for the Indian Removal Act. Under this law, all southern Indians were to be moved to new lands west of the Mississippi River. Congress passed the act in 1830, and President Jackson

From 1838 to 1839 most Cherokee were forced to march west on a "Trail of Tears" that killed 4,000 of them.

signed it. The law also created Indian Territory in what is now the state of Oklahoma. Congress thought that no white people would want this land, so they gave it to the Indians.

The stage was now set for one of the saddest chapters in American history. All of the "five civilized tribes" were to be driven from their homelands and moved to Indian Territory by force. The Cherokees called this journey "the trail where they cried." Today we know it as the "Trail of Tears."

In 1838 President James K. Polk sent General Winfield Scott with 7,000 federal troops to the Cherokee country. The soldiers set up several temporary forts called stockades and ordered all Cherokees to come to these places to be moved west.

Cherokees who did not come in were routed from their homes by soldiers with bayonets. They weren't even allowed to pack their belongings. Most left with only what little they could carry. One Georgia militiaman who was involved in this roundup later became a colonel in the Confederate army. He said, "I fought through the civil war and have seen men shot to pieces and slaughtered by the thousands, but the Cherokee removal was the cruelest work I ever knew."

All the Cherokees' weapons had been taken from them. Still, some resisted. One man named Tsali (called Charley by the whites) was captured along with his wife, brother, and three sons. As they were being driven toward a stockade, the soldiers were so rough on his wife that Tsali told his companions in the Cherokee language, "On my signal, jump on the nearest soldier and take his rifle." In the struggle, one of the rifles went off, and one soldier was killed. The rest of the soldiers ran.

Tsali and his party fled and hid in the cliffs and peaks of the Smoky Mountains. Hundreds of others also escaped to wilderness places. Those who did not starve lived on roots, nuts, and berries. General Scott knew his soldiers could never find them in such a wild area. So he sent a message by the Cherokees' most trusted white friend, Will H. Thomas. He told Tsali if he and his party would surrender, the others could remain "until their case could be adjusted."

Some Cherokees escaped into the Great Smoky Mountains to hide from soldiers.

Tsali turned himself in with his sons and brother. All were executed by a firing squad made up of Cherokees who were forced to shoot their comrades. Only Tsali's youngest son was spared because of his age. The Cherokees who had escaped became the ancestors of the Eastern Band of Cherokee Indians who live in western North Carolina today.

In June 1838, 5,000 Cherokees were loaded onto steamboats at several points along the Tennessee River. The boats took them down the Tennessee to the Ohio River. From there they went down the Ohio to the west side of the Mississippi, where they made the rest of the journey on foot. Many people died from the extreme heat. John Ross asked General Scott to let Cherokee leaders take over the removal. Scott

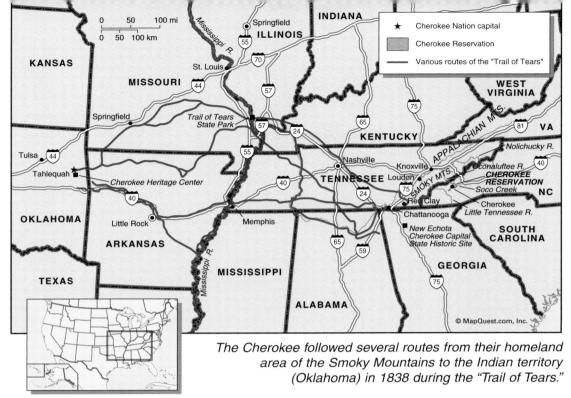

The Cherokee followed several routes from their homeland area of the Smoky Mountains to the Indian territory (Oklahoma) in 1838 during the "Trail of Tears."

agreed but insisted that the rest begin to leave by October 20th.

The 13,000 remaining Cherokee captives began the more than 1,000-mile (1,600-km) overland journey in the fall of 1838. There were 645 wagons in the caravan in which the old, disabled, and small children rode. Those who had horses rode them part of the time. All the rest walked.

The soldiers were anything but kind as they herded the people westward. They did not like their jobs and took their anger out on the Indians. They prodded the slower walkers with bayonets or beat them with rifle butts. Many of the older and weaker people died along the way and were hurriedly buried in unmarked graves. As winter came more and more people died of exposure, especially children. Warm clothing and blankets were scarce. When they reached the Mississippi River, it was full of ice. They had to wait in the bitter cold with no shelter until the ice cleared and they could get across. Here many more died of exposure. In all, more than 4,000 Cherokees died on the trail. This equals about one out of every four who started it.

The Cherokee Way of Life

Clothing

The clothing of the Cherokees, before they met Europeans, was very simple. A man's everyday garment was just a **breech-clout**. This was a piece of very soft deerskin about 20 inches (50 cm) wide and 40 inches (100 cm) long. A man would tie a narrow piece of leather around his waist like a belt. He took one end of the breechclout and brought it up under the belt in front. Then he passed the other end between his legs and brought it up under the belt in back. If he was leaving the village to hunt or for war, he wore moccasins. He also wore leggings to protect his legs from briars and branches. These items were all made of deerskin. In cooler weather, he might also wear a buckskin hunting shirt that reached almost to his knees or a cloak made of wild turkey feathers. Sometimes his cloak was made from animal skins with the fur still on them. He wore the fur on the inside, next to his skin, when it was really cold.

Women's clothes were even simpler than the men's. Women usually wore only a wraparound skirt made of soft deerskin. The skirt reached almost to the knees. Around the village, women went barefoot like the men. Winter moccasins for both men and women covered the leg almost up to the knee. In colder weather women sometimes wore a sort of dress that hung from one shoulder, leaving the other shoulder bare.

Children generally wore nothing at all until they were about ten years old. After that, they wore smaller copies of adult clothes.

When stalking game, a hunter might wrap himself in a fur cloak to ward off the cold.

18

To make comfortable clothes from deerskin was a lot of work. First a skin was stretched on a square frame made of poles. All the meat and fat were scraped from the inside. It was then soaked in a liquid made from one part hickory ashes and two to three parts water. Then the Cherokees squeezed out as much of the liquid as they could and pulled off all the hair. Next the cooked brains of the animal were rubbed into the skin with a smooth stone. Then the skin was pulled back and forth over a very smooth pole until it was almost dry. It was then smoked over a small, smoky fire made from a wood, like pine or cedar, containing resin. This smoking made it **water-repellent**. Even today, this product is called "brain-tanned" buckskin, and it is still in demand.

It took women about 40 hours of work to prepare a deerskin for making clothes. As white traders began to offer them cloth, the Cherokee women were very glad to get it. It saved them a lot of work preparing the skins and was easier to sew into clothes. It also meant there were more skins for trading. The men liked the way cloth clothing looked. Both men and women liked the white man's wool blankets. They soon learned to make the blankets into coats that didn't keep falling off their shoulders like blankets. Oddly enough, while Indians began to wear cloth clothes, many white men began to wear clothing made of deerskin. It lasted longer than cloth and protected them better. Whites usually made the skins into pants and shirts instead of leggings and breechclouts.

Houses

Before the Europeans came, Cherokees lived in two basic styles of houses, one in warm weather and another in cold weather. The "summer houses" were

Morning Star Conner wears a "tear dress," named in a time when scissors were scarce and fabric was ripped to fit.

of different sizes. Some were as big as today's single-width mobile homes. Their shape was much like a mobile home with a **gabled** roof. Often, several related families lived in the same house. These warm-weather buildings were somewhat like the "longhouses" used by their northern cousins, the Iroquois.

The summer house was built by placing posts in the ground every 2 to 3 feet (0.6 to 1 m) in two parallel rows. These rows were 12 to 15 feet (4 to 5 m) apart and as long as the house was to be. Then one smaller post was placed between each pair of large posts. When this step was completed, saplings or split river canes were woven through the main framework. Often clam or mussel shells were ground into a paste to make a sort of whitewash to paint over the outside. The roof framework was much like the sides and was supported by the wall posts. It was covered with slabs of tree bark laid like shingles on top of the framework. A small smoke hole was left in the roof to let out smoke from cooking fires.

The other house was used in cold weather, but it might be called a "hot house." It was much smaller than the summer house and was round, like an upside-down bowl. Framework posts were set into the ground in a circle some 12 to 15 feet

Cherokee summer houses (left) let in cooling breezes; winter houses (below) were built low to keep heat inside.

(4 to 5 m) in diameter. Saplings or split canes were woven through the framework in much the same way as in the longhouse. The dirt floor was dug down about a foot below the surface. The roof framework was made strong enough to support a lot of weight. A mixture of clay, with some grass added for strength, was smeared over the framework of the roof and side walls. This mixture was 6 to 7 inches (15 to 18 cm) thick. When dry it kept out the cold quite well. Almost all families had both a summer house and a hot house. By about 1775, however, most Cherokee families lived in log cabins, and by 1800, some Cherokees had even built frame or brick "plantation houses," similar to ones owned by their white neighbors.

By the early 1800s, Cherokees began to live in log cabins.

Foods

When the Europeans arrived, the Cherokees' diet was about as **varied** as that of any American Indians. They ate venison (deer meat), bear, rabbit, squirrel, wild turkey, grouse, quail, wild ducks, and many kinds of fish. They also grew many different vegetables.

The Cherokees called their main vegetables the "three sisters." These were corn, beans, and squash. To plant them, the ground was broken a little with a bone or wood hoe, and a small hill was prepared. Five or six seeds were dropped into each hill about 2 inches (5 cm) apart and covered with earth. The hills were usually about 3 feet (1 m) apart in straight rows. The Cherokees grew corn, beans, squash, pumpkins, gourds, sunflowers, and tobacco. Tobacco was considered

Clay pots were good for many uses including cooking stews.

sacred by nearly all Indians, including the Cherokees.

The "three sisters" were normally planted in large fields. Each **clan**, or group of related families, worked its own section. The men and boys helped prepare the ground. After the crop was planted, the women and girls did most of the garden tending. Every family in the village shared in that harvest according to their needs. Most families also had a small garden plot beside their house. Here they grew vegetables just for their own family. Meats were usually roasted on a spit over the fire or made into a stew with vegetables. These were cooked with water in a clay pot.

Games

Both Cherokee children and adults loved to play games. Some games were very active and exciting. Some, like "chunkey" (page 43) were quieter.

The most exciting game was one they called "little brother to war." This game of **stickball** was played all over the Southeast by one town or one tribe against another. It was somewhat like the game of lacrosse that was played by tribes in the Northeast.

Every stickball player carried two sticks, each about 2.5 feet (.7 m) long. At one end of each stick was a small basket made of leather thongs woven into a sort of webbing. The Cherokee ball was made of deerskin stuffed with deer hair. It was smaller than a lacrosse ball and slightly smaller than a modern golf ball.

At each end of the large, level field was a goal. It was much like today's football goalposts but narrower and taller. To score a point, a team must carry the ball between the uprights and under the crossbar of the goalposts. Among the Cherokees, a game usually ended when one team had scored 12 points. Some games lasted all day.

Players prepared for a game much like they prepared for war. First they would **fast** for three days. Then they would go into the **asi**, or sweat lodge, for several hours. Next they plunged into a cold stream. This purified the outer man. They then drank a mixture called the "black drink," which made them throw up everything in their stomachs. That purified the inner man. Next, the **conjurer** would take a snake tooth comb and scratch the players' arms and upper body until they were covered with blood. This was to make them look fierce to their opponents.

Stickball was a very rough game. The only real rule was that a player had to control the ball with his sticks. If he wished to

To play stickball, a player had two sticks, one to carry the ball in, the other to defend himself.

hit an opponent with his stick, he could, but he made sure not to hit so hard that his stick broke. Players often got hurt, and some got killed. It was almost as great an honor to be hurt or killed in a stickball game as in war. Modern Cherokees still play stickball, but with many more rules. Serious injuries are rare today.

Boys played games that prepared them to become hunters and warriors. They learned to make their own bows and arrows. Bows were usually made of honey locust or hickory, and arrows of river cane. Boys also learned to make blowguns out of river cane. The darts for this weapon were made of locust and were **fletched** with thistle down. Blowguns were used to hunt small game such as rabbits, birds, and squirrels. Boys also ran **footraces** and had shooting contests with their bows, arrows, and blowguns. A boy was not considered ready to hunt until he could hit a rabbit in the eye with a dart from a blowgun.

The girls' favorite toys were dolls made from cornhusks. These they treated like their mothers treated children. Both boys and girls played such childhood games as tag and hide-and-go-seek.

Corn husk dolls are still popular with children.

Arts and Crafts

Cherokee women made some of the best baskets in the whole country. They used very thin strips of river cane, oak, or maple. Some baskets were for storage, some for carrying food, some for carrying loads.

Woven baskets were often used to store or carry food.

Basket makers also wove mats from river cane. These, too, had many different uses. They were used to cover seats and beds and to hang over doorways.

The Cherokees knew how to weave simple fabrics from certain vegetable fibers and animal hair. These fabrics were generally used to make sashes, caps, garters, and shirts.

Human and animal figures were, and still are, carved from both wood and stone. Some were made into pipes, and some were just for decoration.

Another art form common among the Cherokees was that of carving **gorgets** and **medallions** on mussel

Weaver Molly Taylor Little John crafts a belt from natural fibers.

shells. One of the most common designs was two circles, one just inside another, with a cross in the center of the two. The circles represented Mother Earth. The cross divided the circles into four equal parts that stood for the four directions: north, south, east, and west.

This medallion represents Mother Earth and the four directions, north, east, south, and west.

Religion and Medicine

Cherokee medicine men were both doctors and priests. The Cherokees called these men, and sometimes women, conjurers. To appreciate Cherokee **spirituality**, there are some ideas one must understand. Cherokees believed that every living thing—not just human beings—had a spirit made by God. For example, before a Cherokee hunter killed a deer, he first gave thanks to

Before killing a deer, a hunter gave thanks to the animal for feeding his family and promised not to waste any part of the deer.

the deer's spirit. He thanked it for giving up its life to help feed and clothe him and his family. Next he promised the deer's spirit that no part of its body would be wasted; every single part would be used in some way.

Of course, the deer's flesh (venison) was eaten. Its bones were used to make needles, **awls**, fishhooks, and many other useful items. The hide was treated with the deer's brains to make clothing and moccasins. Or the hide was used untreated, as rawhide. With the hair left on, it was used for bedding or cloaks. Thin strips of sinew, a tendon along either side of the backbone, was used for all kinds of sewing. Rawhide handles attached to gourds made them into pails. These were used to store and carry liquids such as water, honey, and bear oil for cooking. Even the hollowed-out deer hooves were tied around men's knees to make noise as they danced. The inside of the hooves were made into glue. The antlers of a male deer were made into tools to chip flint or into points for weapons. Cherokees wasted nothing.

They felt surrounded by the spirits of all the birds, animals, fish, trees, and plants. They found it natural to value those spirits highly. They believed that God, the Creator, used the spirits of animals, birds, or plants to bring them messages. Sometimes the message the spirit brought was good. Sometimes it was a warning that something bad was about to happen.

Dreams were very important to all Indian people, and the Cherokees were no exception. Most often they believed messages from the spirit world came to them in their dreams. If they didn't understand the message of a dream, they would tell the dream to the conjurer. The conjurer would explain it for them.

Cherokees sometimes referred to their **deity** as "The Elder Fires Above." These seem to have been three in number. One was U ha lo te ga, meaning "head of all power." Another was A tu nu ti tsu to li tsi ti, meaning "place of uniting." The third was U s go u la, meaning "place below the breast." Later, white missionaries began to tell Cherokees about the Father, Son, and Holy Spirit. This seemed to fit with what they already believed.

Goingback Chiltoskey, a respected elder, carves an eagle, long a symbol of power and freedom to the Cherokee people.

Perhaps this is the reason so many Cherokees quickly accepted Christianity. Many of today's Cherokees believe in both their traditional religion and Christianity. "Why not?" they ask. "It's the same God, the Creator."

The conjurer was also the village doctor. He healed the sick and injured with both **herbs** and **formulas**. He gave the patient medicines made from plants and herbs gathered in

Walker Calhoun and his grandson, Patrick, collect witch hazel to make medicinal tea.

the mountains and valleys. He also recited or sang the sacred formulas that had been handed down for generations. This often convinced the patient that he or she would recover. Today's doctors call this **holistic** medicine, and it is sometimes quite effective.

Another treatment for the sick was the asi. This was a small, round building very like the hot house but with a much smaller doorway. The floor was about a foot below the level of the ground. There was a bench all around the inner walls on which the people sat. Stones were heated outside in a fire, then brought into the asi and placed in a shallow pit in the center. Water was sprinkled over the hot rocks with a special gourd dipper. This made clouds of steam. The asi was also where the conjurers held instruction for those who were chosen to learn the conjurer's art.

Cherokees had no special day, like Sunday, for religion. They prayed many times every day whenever they felt prayer was needed. As soon as they got up each morning, before eating any food, everyone was expected to "go to water." This was

done to keep both the body and the spirit cleansed. They went to a bend in a stream where the upstream direction was east. As they finished bathing facing the rising sun, they thanked the Creator for the new day.

The numbers four and seven were, and still are, sacred to the Cherokees. These numbers occur again and again in Cherokee traditions.

Four comes from the four directions. From these points Earth was hung from the Sky Rock. Each direction is associated with a certain color. East is represented by red, south by white, west by black, and north by blue.

The importance of seven comes from the seven levels of the Upper World, each being a better place than the one below it. The seventh, or highest, level was seldom, if ever, reached by any human. The number seven is also connected to the legend of the Sun. When the Sun was first made, it hung much lower than it does now, and the world was too hot. So the conjurers kept moving it up a **handbreadth** at a time until it was seven handbreadths above the Earth. There it made its daily journey just below the dome of the Sky Rock. Then it was just right, and it remains so to this day.

Leaves turn almost as yellow as the Sun itself in Great Smoky Mountains National Park.

Family Life

Clans

Almost every part of Cherokee life revolved around the clan system. Everyone to whom one had any blood relation through their mother was a member of the same clan. Cherokee society was **matrilineal,** which means ancestry was traced through the mother, not the father. Thus, when a man married, he went to live with his wife's people. Also, all children became members of their mother's clan, not their father's clan.

The Cherokees had, and still have, seven clans. They are: Bird Clan, Deer Clan, Red Paint Clan, Blue Clan, Wild Potato Clan, Wolf Clan, and Long Hair Clan. In any town, members of the same clan lived near one another. People were not allowed to marry anyone from their own clans.

Childhood

For Cherokee children, childhood was truly a happy time. Parents believed that it should be a fun time as well as a learning time. As long as children showed proper respect for adults, especially elders, they could do as they wished.

Thomas Muskrat and his grandson, Justin, turn out in full regalia for an Oklahoma powwow.

Since a boy was not a member of his father's clan, he was not taught the skills he would need as an adult hunter and warrior by his father. Instead, those skills were usually taught by an uncle, a brother of his mother's. Most discipline was handled by a few sharp words from an elder. On those rare occasions when a boy needed physical punishment, it came from his uncle, not his father.

A girl's training was up to her mother and aunts because they were members of the same clan. Girls began to help adults with household tasks at a very early age. Younger girls usually helped with housekeeping chores. These included taking

Lorene Drywater sews ribbon shirts, makes buffalo grass dolls, and passes her skills to her granddaughters.

care of younger brothers and sisters or working in the family garden plots. Older girls did such jobs as carrying water to the house, cooking, and helping to "brain-tan" skins and make clothing.

Courtship and Marriage

When a young man in his late teens liked a particular girl, he had an easy way to let her know it. He watched to see where she went each day for the family's water supply. Then he sat along the path she usually took. When she came along, he played the courting flute for her. If she liked him, she smiled. That meant he could come visit her at her mother's house that night. If she didn't like him, she would stick her nose in the air and act as if he were not there. When that happened, he could either choose another girl or practice the flute more.

When a young girl liked a particular boy, she would cook a nice hot bowl of food. She set it out where she thought he would pass by. If he ate it, they would start seeing each other. If he didn't, she chose another boy. If the wrong boy tried to eat it, she chased him away.

When a young couple had chosen each other, the boy's mother and the girl's mother would get together and talk. This was to make sure both families approved of the marriage. If they did (and they usually did), the groom would build a house for his bride. Then they could be married. The house would be hers from then on, no matter what happened.

When a woman wanted a divorce, she gathered up all of her husband's belongings and placed them in a pile outside her door. He then knew the marriage was ended and went home to his mother's house.

If a man wanted a divorce, he simply gathered up his belongings and left. Both man and woman were immediately free to remarry. While divorce was easy, it was not common. In all cases, children stayed with their mother.

Tribal Life

Government

The basic form of Cherokee government was the same whether it was for one town or for the entire nation. Like almost everything in Cherokee life, it was based on the clan system.

Each town had both a peace chief and a war chief. When the Cherokees were at peace, the peace chief was in charge. When they took the warpath, the war chief was their leader. The peace chief was responsible for ceremonies, religion, settling disputes, and the day-to-day operation of the government. The peace chief normally dressed all in white for special occasions. The war chief wore all red clothing at special events. Both chiefs were members of the town council.

The town council was made up of seven highly respected elders, one from each of the seven clans. There was also a Council of Seven Women, also one from each clan. Their leader was known as the Most Beloved Woman. She was chosen for her character and her good

The headdresses of peace chiefs were adorned in brilliant white, while war chiefs wore red.

works. She, like the two chiefs, was a member of the town council. This same pattern of government was followed in Echota, the Cherokee capital, for the whole nation. Neither the chiefs nor the councils had great power. They governed by trying to reach a general agreement.

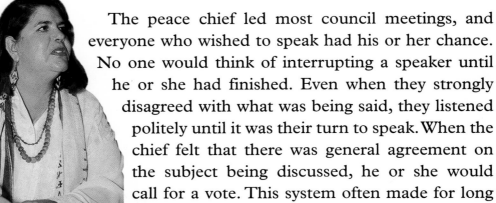

In 1987 Wilma Mankiller became the first woman to be elected Principal Chief of the Cherokee Nation.

The peace chief led most council meetings, and everyone who wished to speak had his or her chance. No one would think of interrupting a speaker until he or she had finished. Even when they strongly disagreed with what was being said, they listened politely until it was their turn to speak. When the chief felt that there was general agreement on the subject being discussed, he or she would call for a vote. This system often made for long meetings, but it also caused people to feel good about decisions. They had heard all sides of the question and had been able to vote on it. Votes were usually **unanimous**. The individual towns were quite independent and did not always follow the policies of the national council. This confused and frustrated the Europeans because they expected national governments to have complete power over all their people.

In good weather, ceremonies and meetings were held in the "Stomp Ground," or dance area, beside the seven-sided council house. In the Cherokee capital, Echota, the council house could seat more than 500 people. A pie-shaped section was reserved for each clan. The floor sloped from the walls down to a flat area in the center. This looked much like the bleachers used today for sporting events. The chiefs and council members sat in the level area in the center of the building, where the sacred fire burned all day and night.

Ceremonies

Ceremonies, which often included dancing, were, and still are, a very important part of Cherokee life. Whenever important visitors came to town, they were welcomed by the Eagle Dance.

As with most southeastern tribes, the Green Corn Ceremony was the most important ceremony of the year. This was celebrated when the corn in the large fields was ripe enough to eat. Its purpose was to thank the Creator for another harvest that would feed the people through the coming winter.

Messengers were sent out to tell all the people in the various villages of the event. They picked seven ears of new corn, one from each clan's field, and brought them to the peace chief. The chief and seven council members fasted for six days after the corn was brought to them. This allowed time for the people to gather. Everyone stayed awake the sixth night, and the ceremony started at daybreak on the seventh day. The peace chief said a prayer thanking the Creator for the corn. Taking kernels

Elaborate movements of the Eagle Dance shown here once welcomed important visitors. They are still performed in North Carolina at the pageant called "Unto These Hills."

from the seven ears of corn, he placed them on a deer's tongue and laid them in the sacred fire. Sacred tobacco was then sprinkled into the sacred fire. Food from the new corn was prepared and eaten by everyone except the peace chief and seven council members. They could not eat any of the new corn for seven more days, but they could eat corn from the previous year's crop.

A unique Cherokee ceremony called the Booger Dance was used to make fun of things they either feared, like diseases, or disliked, like Europeans. Men came bursting into an area where the people were gathered. Dancers dressed in ragged clothes and wore masks covering their faces. Masks represented the things or people they wanted to **ridicule**. For example, a mask for smallpox was made from a hornets' nest. The wrinkled surface of the mask looked and felt like the awful scars this disease left

A mask made of a hornets' nest was used in the "Booger Dance."

on its victims who survived. The dancers were usually quite rude, even crude, yet no one was offended.

Masks were also used in dances performed before a hunting trip. The masks were for deer, bear, and the eastern buffalo (before these were all killed) and were thought to make these animals come to the hunters. Prayers were also said to ask the spirits of these animals to give themselves to the hunters.

The Forks of the Road

The Eastern Band of Cherokee Indians

The Eastern Band of Cherokee Indians, now living in western North Carolina, owe their continuing existence there to a white man. His name was William Holland Thomas or Wil-Usdi, which means "Little Will" in Cherokee.

The last group of Cherokees started west on the Trail of Tears in December 1838. Nine months later it was reported that about 1,000 Cherokees remained scattered in the mountains of North Carolina and Tennessee. This group was led by one of the Eastern Cherokees' greatest chiefs, Yonaguska (Drowning Bear), the adopted father of Will Thomas. Yonaguska acquired some land in the area now called the Qualla Boundary, along the Oconaluftee River and Soco Creek. It is from these people that the Eastern or Qualla Band of Cherokees are descended.

The Cherokee Reservation is not really a reservation at all. Almost all other Indian reservations in the United States are provided by either a state or by the federal government. The Indians don't own the land they live on. If the government chose to break another treaty, as it has many times, it could force the reservation Indians to leave. It cannot do this to the Qualla Cherokees, who actually own the land most people call the Cherokee Reservation. This is unusual because their ancestors did not believe people could own a part of the earth, the air, the sky, or the sea. They believed those things belonged to the Creator, who put them there for all His children to enjoy.

Here is how the Eastern Cherokees became owners of their land. William Holland Thomas was a white man who owned a trading post. He was liked, trusted, and respected by the Cherokee. So when Chief Yonaguska learned Thomas's own father had died before Will was born, he adopted Will as his son. From then on, Wil-usdi' was regarded by the Cherokees as their brother.

When Yonaguska died, Thomas became chief of the Eastern Cherokees. After countless trips to Washington, D.C. over many years, he finally convinced the U.S. government to agree to pay these Cherokees their share of the "removal money" it had paid to those who had gone to Oklahoma.

Thomas planned to help the eastern Cherokees buy land on which to live. By the time Thomas died, North Carolina had accepted the Cherokees as citizens. But the Bureau of Indian Affairs still holds the Qualla Boundary land in trust for the Cherokees. This means that the Cherokees cannot sell the land, but neither can the federal government. Thanks to Wil-usdi', his adopted people can remain in their beloved homeland forever.

Cherokee, North Carolina, is a vacation destination for many Americans today. It has many interesting tourist attractions such

Craftspeople demonstrate a wide range of talent from basketmaking, beadwork, fingerweaving, to wood carving and pottery making at the recreated 1750s community at Oconaluftee Indian Village.

as the Museum of the Cherokee Indian, the Cherokee Heritage Museum, Oconaluftee Village, and the outdoor drama "Unto These Hills," which retells the story of Tsali's sacrifice for his people. There are also several shops where handcrafts made by Cherokees can be purchased.

The Cherokee Nation

Under the Treaty of New Echota, a minority of Cherokees had agreed to sell their homeland to the U.S. government. They got the best deal they could from the United States and moved to Indian Territory voluntarily. The group set up a tribal government in what is now the state of Oklahoma.

When the majority of the Cherokees arrived in Indian Territory in the spring of 1839, at the end of the Trail of Tears, they were not warmly received. The main body of the Cherokees felt that the minority group who had signed the Treaty of New Echota had broken an important law. There were many hard feelings between the two **factions**. Three leaders of the "1835 treaty signers" were assassinated by supporters of the other faction.

In spite of all the pain and suffering the U.S. government had caused the Cherokees, government agents did try to calm tempers and unite the two factions. On July 12, 1839, a general convention of the two groups was held. This convention passed an act of union bringing together the "new arrivals" and the "old settlers" to form the "Cherokee Nation."

The original Cherokee constitution was modified to fit new circumstances. A central tribal government has legislative, executive, and judicial branches much like the U.S. government.

Just as things were calming down between the former factions of the Cherokees and their other Indian neighbors, the

American Civil War broke out. John Ross, the principal chief, urged the Cherokees not to take sides but to remain neutral. But one faction supported the Confederacy, since many Cherokees owned black slaves. The other faction supported the Union. Most Cherokee men enlisted in the Confederate Army, but a substantial number chose to fight in the Union Army.

Oklahoma became a bloody battleground. Five years of war left the Cherokees with their numbers reduced from 21,000 to 14,000 and their country in ashes. The homes, farms, and public buildings they had built over the previous 20 years were mostly destroyed by one army or the other. The Cherokees had to rebuild again.

Confederate Cherokee regiments charge a Union line in Arkansas during the Civil War. Many other Cherokees fought for the Union.

Modern Cherokee Life

Cherokees today are faced with three choices. They can adopt white ways and give up their own culture; withdraw from society and live as hermits; or learn to "live in two worlds." Most choose the third way. They live in the white world part of the time and in the Indian world the rest of the time. Fortunately, there are enough elders still living to teach the Indian way of life to the younger generation.

If Indians are going to enjoy any financial success, they have to play by the white man's rules. That's where the money is. They live in homes as much like those of whites as they can afford. They dress in the same type of clothing whites wear.

They participate in intertribal pow-wows, where a sort of all-Indian culture is developing.

In the east, the town of Cherokee, North Carolina, is the hub for some 11,500 enrolled members in the Eastern Band of Cherokee Indians. The vast majority of these live on the Qualla Boundary. Here the offices of the chief, vice chief, and tribal council are located. A hospital is operated by the U.S. Indian Health Service, while the elementary and high schools are operated by the tribe itself. The Cherokee language is now being taught in those schools.

A student drills to learn the Cherokee language including the syllabary invented by Sequoyah.

Many Eastern Cherokees have found employment in growing industries. Many others work for the tribal government as police officers, firefighters, teachers, hospital workers, and office workers. Others work in jobs related to the tourist industry, which booms in the spring, summer, and fall.

The tribe owns two small industries. One makes Indian items for the tourist trade. The other makes mirrors.

In 1994 the tribe opened a small gambling casino in Cherokee, which has given jobs to Cherokees and cash income to each person on the tribal roll. A huge gambling casino planned in Cherokee will be managed by an outside

Making and painting pottery provides income to Cherokee people and treasures to visitors.

corporation. Whether this source of income will turn out to be a blessing or a curse is still unknown. Only time will tell.

In the west, Tahlequah, Oklahoma, is the historic and present capital of the Cherokee Nation. There you can find the tribal offices and a fine museum, cultural center, tribal library, model village, and an outdoor theater.

Most of the Cherokee people in Oklahoma who live within driving distance of the larger towns and cities get much better paying and more permanent jobs than those living in rural areas. Even so, the unemployment rate for Cherokees, both eastern and western, is three to four times that of the rest of the United States. And, because they have less education than the average white person, more of them have to work at hard, low-paying jobs.

In April 1984 a joint meeting of the leaders of the Cherokee Nation from Oklahoma and the Eastern Band of Cherokees

from North Carolina was held at Red Clay, Tennessee. There, more than 150 years ago, the last meeting of the National Council was held before the forced march of the Trail of Tears.

Will the two forks of the Cherokee road come back together and join as one nation? Many people hope so, but it is unlikely. There are just too many miles between the Qualla Boundary in North Carolina and Tahlequah, Oklahoma.

In 1984 the Eastern Band of Cherokee Indians, Robert Youngdeer, Chief, (left) and the Cherokee Nation, Ross Swimmer, Chief (right) held a joint council for the first time since before the "Trail of Tears."

The Game of Chunkey

Equipment needed

1. A level strip of earth, preferably bare of grass. This strip should be approximately 75 to 100 feet (23 to 30 m) long and 10 feet (3 m) wide. A level sidewalk also works well. (This is the "alley" for rolling the "stone.") A "foul" line, perpendicular to the alley, is marked off on either side of the alley about five steps from the starting end. The players must not cross the foul line.

2. Two lengths of rope or highly visible string as long as the "alley"; one is laid along each edge to mark the "alley."

3. An old broomstick for each player. Players may decorate their sticks if they wish.

4. A solid wood circle, 1 inch (3 cm) thick and 8 inches (20 cm) in diameter, can serve as a chunkey stone. An old wheel from a toy wagon or tricycle also works well.

Stick and stones used in playing Chunkey

Playing the game

Two players are selected. They start four steps behind the foul line, one on either side of the alley.

A third person, (the roller) rolls the chunkey stone down the alley away from the players, just hard enough so it will stop rolling before it reaches the other end of the alley. A judge makes sure no player steps on or crosses the foul line. If either player steps on or crosses the foul line, that player is disqualified, and the other player gets the points.

As soon as the stone is released, the players may start forward. They must throw their sticks down the alley before reaching the foul line and while the stone is still rolling. If a player hits the rolling stone with his stick, he scores 2 points. If neither player hits the rolling stone, the player whose stick is nearest to where the stone stops rolling and falls over scores 1 point. The first player to score 7 points wins the game.

Cherokee Chronology

Before 1400	The Cherokee tribe may have originated near modern Pittsburgh, Pennsylvania.
1540	First contact with Europeans in the person of Spanish explorer Hernando de Soto.
1629	Cornelius Dougherty, a trader and Irishman, comes to live with the Cherokees.
1730	Seven chiefs and subchiefs visit England and meet with the King.
1776–1783	The Cherokees support Britain during the American Revolution.
1809	Sequoyah develops a Cherokee system of writing.
1814	Cherokee warriors help General Andrew Jackson defeat Creek Indians in battle.
1829	Gold is discovered on Cherokee lands in Georgia.
1830	Andrew Jackson, now President, signs the Indian Removal Act, which also creates Indian Territory in Oklahoma.
1838	Federal troops force the Cherokees from their homes and send them to Oklahoma on the "Trail of Tears." About 1,000 escape into the Eastern woodlands.
1861–1865	Cherokees in Oklahoma split their loyalty in the Civil War. Some fight for the Union; more fight for the Confederacy.
1870s–1970s	The Cherokee Nation of Oklahoma and the Eastern Band of Cherokees from North Carolina remain separated and suffer under changing government policies toward Indians.
1984	Leaders of the Cherokee Nation and Eastern Band meet officially for the first time in 150 years.
1994	The Eastern Band opens a small gaming casino in the town of Cherokee.

Glossary

Asi A sweat lodge.

Awl A pointed tool used to make holes in leather.

Breechclout A loincloth often worn by Cherokee men.

Clan A group claiming a common ancestor.

Conjurer A Cherokee religious leader and healer.

Deity Supreme being or God.

Epidemic The rapid spreading of a disease.

Faction A group or clique within a larger group, party, government, or organization.

Fast To go without eating.

Fletch To put feathers on an arrow or dart.

Footraces A race run by humans on foot.

Foreign From another country or area.

Formula A fixed form or sequence of words.

Gable A high-pitched roof with sloping sides.

Gorget An ornament worn at the throat.

Handbreadth A unit of measure based on the width of a human hand. It can vary from 2.5 to 4 inches (6.4 to 10 cm).

Herb A plant with leaves, stems, seeds, or roots that are used for medicine or for flavor in cooking or for fragrance.

Holistic Involving the body, mind, and spirit.

Immunity Resistance to a disease.

Matrilineal Tracing ancestry through the mother.

Medallion A round ornament or design.

Militia Citizens of a state trained to fight in emergencies.

Radical Favoring extreme change.

Ridicule To make someone or something look foolish.

Spirituality Dealing with the spirit or soul.

Stickball A game somewhat like lacrosse that was played by northern tribes except each player has two racquets (sticks) and the ball is much smaller.

Syllabary A system of symbols representing spoken sounds.

Testify To make a statement after promising to tell the truth. In court, witnesses testify when giving evidence.

Tsalagi (or Ani Kituwah) The name the Cherokee give themselves. Ani Kituwah means "people of Kituwah."

Unanimous In or showing total agreement.

Varied Of different kinds.

Water-repellent Almost waterproof.

The author of this book, Herb McAmis, is shown here in a costume he wears as a southern plains straight dancer.

Further Reading

Burt, Jesse, and Robert B. Ferguson. *Indians of the Southeast: Then and Now.* Nashville and New York: Abingdon Press, 1973.

Cotterill, R.S. *The Southeastern Indians: The Story of the Civilized Tribes Before Removal.* Norman: University of Oklahoma Press, 1954.

Glassman, Bruce. *Wilma Mankiller: Chief of the Cherokee Nation.* Blackbirch Press, 1992.

Grumet, Robert S. *The Lenapes.* New York and Philadelphia: Chelsea House, 1989.

Hudson, Charles. *The Southeastern Indians.* Knoxville: University of Tennessee Press, 1976.

Lowe, Felix C. *John Ross.* Austin: Raintree Steck-Vaughn, 1991.

Mancini, Richard E. *Indians of the Southeast.* New York: Facts On File, 1992.

McClure, Tony Mack. *Cherokee Proud.* Somerville, Tennessee: Chuanannee Books, 1999.

Mooney, James. *Myths of the Cherokee and Sacred Formulas of the Cherokee.* Nashville: Charles Elder, 1972.

Nabokov, Peter. *Native American Testimony.* Middlesex, England: Viking Press, 1991.

Perdue, Theda. *The Cherokee.* New York: Chelsea House, 1989.

Satz, Ronald N. *Tennessee's Indian People.* Knoxville: University of Tennessee Press, 1979.

Scheer, George F. *Cherokee Animal Tales.* Tulsa: Council Oaks Books, 1968.

Viola, Herman J. *North American Indians: An Introduction to the Lives of America's Native Peoples, from the Inuit of the Arctic to the Zuni of the Southwest.* Crown Publishers, 1996.

Index

Numbers in italics indicate illustration or map.